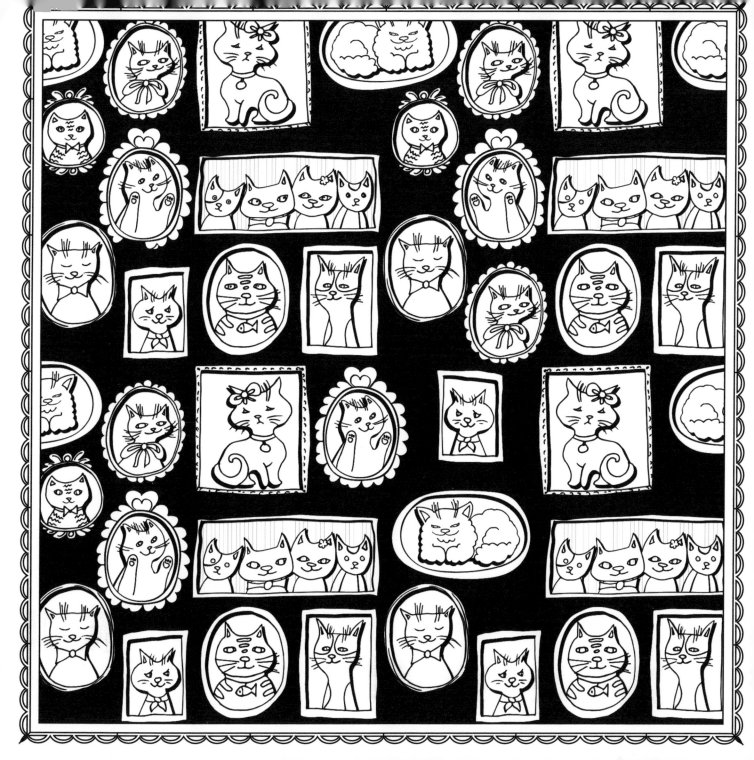

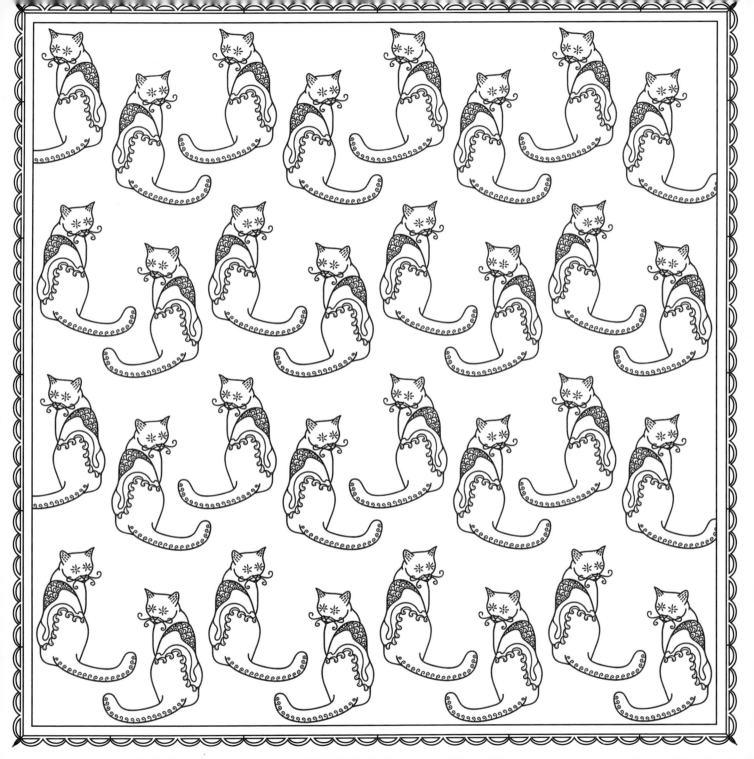

First edition for North America, the Philippines, Singapore, Malaysia, and Japan published in 2016 by Barron's Educational Series, Inc.

Original German title: *Katzenglück*
© Copyright 2016 arsEdition GmbH, München

ISBN: 978-1-4380-0930-8
www.barronseduc.com

All inquiries should be addressed to:
Barron's Educational Series, Inc.
250 Wireless Boulevard
Hauppauge, NY 11788

Interior Design: Eva Schindler,
Atelier für grafische Gestaltung
Cover Design: Getty Images/Thinkstock: iStockphoto:
tigra62; Firbus Mara/Shutterstock
Illustrations: Getty Images/Thinkstock; Fotolia: (IP),
Kudryashka, meduzzza, Oksana, tablizan
Printed in China
9 8 7 6 5 4 3 2

RELAX, CREATE, AND DREAM WITH COLORING BOOKS AND PADS!

Color Magic Series

MOTIF MAGIC
ISBN 978-1-4380-0794-6

MAGIC GOLD
ISBN 978-1-4380-0847-9

Color Magic to Frame & Display

THE MAGIC OF MANDALAS
ISBN 978-1-4380-7683-6

THE MAGIC OF FLOWERS
ISBN 978-1-4380-7684-3

Pads of Color

LAUGH LOVE LIVE
ISBN 978-1-4380-0900-1

MAGIC OF FLOWERS & BIRDS
ISBN 978-1-4380-0901-8

MANDALA DREAMS
ISBN 978-1-4380-0902-5

Find more best-selling coloring books at
www.barronseduc.com